D0579757

Teen Life Among the Amish and Other Alternative Communities

Choosing a Lifestyle

Youth in Rural North America

Title List

Getting Ready for the Fair: Crafts, Projects, and Prize-Winning Animals

Growing Up on a Farm: Responsibilities and Issues

Migrant Youth: Falling Between the Cracks

Rural Crime and Poverty: Violence, Drugs, and Other Issues

Rural Teens and Animal Raising: Large and Small Pets

Rural Teens and Nature: Conservation and Wildlife Rehabilitation

Rural Teens on the Move:
Cars, Motorcycles, and Off-Road Vehicles

Teen Life Among the Amish and Other Alternative Communities:
Choosing a Lifestyle

Teen Life on Reservations and in First Nation Communities:
Growing Up Native

Teen Minorities in Rural North America: Growing Up Different

Teens and Rural Education: Opportunities and Challenges

Teens and Rural Sports: Rodeos, Horses, Hunting, and Fishing

Teens Who Make a Difference in Rural Communities:
Youth Outreach Organizations and Community Action

Teen Life Among the Amish and Other Alternative Communities
Choosing a Lifestyle

by David Hunter

Mason Crest Publishers

Philadelphia

Mason Crest Publishers Inc.
370 Reed Road
Broomall, Pennsylvania 19008
(866) MCP-BOOK (toll free)
www.masoncrest.com

First printing
1 2 3 4 5 6 7 8 9 10
ISBN 978-1-4222-0011-7 (series)

      Library of Congress Cataloging-in-Publication Data

Hunter, David.
   Teen life among the Amish and other alternative communities :
choosing a lifestyle / by David Hunter.
      p. cm. — (Youth in rural North America)
   Includes bibliographical references (p. 93) and index.
   ISBN 978-1-4222-0017-9
   1. Amish youth—Juvenile literature. 2. Rural youth—United States
—Juvenile literature. 3. Collective settlements—United States
—Juvenile literature.   I. Title. II. Series.
   BX8129.A6H86 2007
   289.70835—dc22
                                     2005032463

Cover and interior design by MK Bassett-Harvey.
Produced by Harding House Publishing Service, Inc.
www.hardinghousepages.com

Cover image design by Peter Spires Culotta.
Cover photography by iStock Photography (Diane Diederich,
   Cindy Haggerty and Daniel Defabio).
Printed in Malaysia by Phoenix Press.

May 2009

Contents

Introduction

by Celeste Carmichael

Results of a survey published by the Kellogg Foundation reveal that most people consider growing up in the country to be idyllic. And it's true that growing up in a rural environment does have real benefits. Research indicates that families in rural areas consistently have more traditional values, and communities are more closely knit. Rural youth spend more time than their urban counterparts in contact with agriculture and nature. Often youth are responsible for gardens and farm animals, and they benefit from both their sense of responsibility and their understanding of the natural world. Studies also indicate that rural youth are more engaged in their communities, working to improve society and local issues. And let us not forget the psychological and aesthetic benefits of living in a serene rural environment!

The advantages of rural living cannot be overlooked—but neither can the challenges. Statistics from around the country show that children in a rural environment face many of the same difficulties that are typically associated with children living in cities, and they fare worse than urban kids on several key indicators of positive youth development. For example, rural youth are more likely than their urban counterparts to use drugs and alcohol. Many of the problems facing rural youth are exacerbated by isolation, lack of jobs (for both parents and teens), and lack of support services for families in rural communities.

When most people hear the word "rural," they instantly think "farms." Actually, however, less than 12 percent of the population in rural areas make their livings through agriculture. Instead, service jobs are the top industry in rural North America. The lack of opportunities for higher paying jobs can trigger many problems: persistent poverty, lower educational standards, limited access to health care, inadequate housing, underemployment of teens, and lack of extracurricular possibilities. Additionally, the lack of—or in some cases surge of—diverse populations in rural communities presents its own set of challenges for youth and communities. All these concerns lead to the greatest threat to rural communities: the mass exodus of the post–high school population. Teens relocate for educational, recreational, and job opportunities, leaving their hometown indefinitely deficient in youth capital.

This series of books offers an in-depth examination of both the pleasures and challenges for rural youth. Understanding the realities is the first step to expanding the options for rural youth and increasing the likelihood of positive youth development.

CHAPTER 1
An Introduction to Community

Anyone who watches the news or reads the newspaper will probably hear or see the word "community" fairly frequently. Sometimes when people talk about their community, they're talking about the neighborhood in which they live—a place or the people who live in that place. For example, they might say, "St. Augustine is the oldest European community in the United States." In that case, they're talking about a place. On the other hand, they might say, "St. Augustine is a friendly community." Clearly, they're not talking about a place, because people don't think of a place as friendly, regardless of how nice it may be. In this case, they're talking about the people who live in St. Augustine.

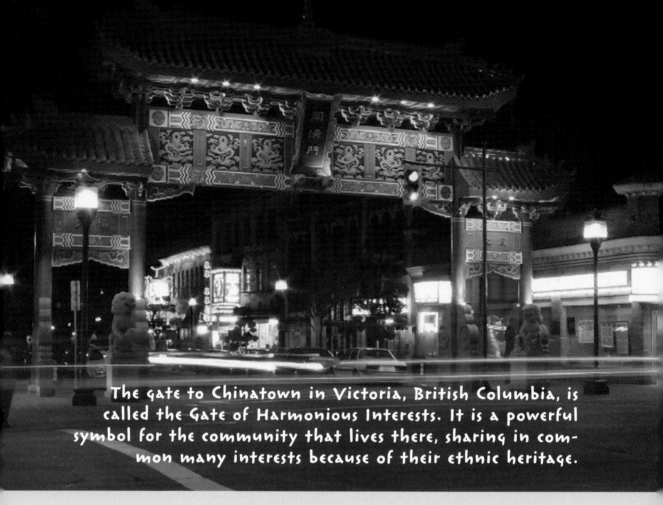

The gate to Chinatown in Victoria, British Columbia, is called the Gate of Harmonious Interests. It is a powerful symbol for the community that lives there, sharing in common many interests because of their ethnic heritage.

"Community" may be used in a much different way, however. Sometimes communities are not places—for example, the business community, the Chinese community, the Muslim community. These don't refer to places, but rather, to people.

Though the word "community" can refer to a place, it more often refers to a group of people, more specifically, to a group of people who share something in common. When someone says "the business community," that person is talking about people involved in business. Other people may be more specific by saying "the Vancouver business community" or "the New York business community," but in both cases, people are still referring to those individuals who are involved in business.

Similarly, "the Chinese community" refers to people of Chinese origin. This may appear in a newspaper in reference to a specific place. For example, "the San Francisco Chinese community" refers to people of Chinese origin who live in San Francisco.

All Chinese people in San Francisco have their ethnic origin in common. All Muslim people in Toronto share something in common—their religion. And all businesspeople in Vancouver and New York are involved in business.

Sharing similar concerns, then, is the essence of community. It is not simply living in close proximity to each other. People who live in the same area also have certain things in common. For example, they might want to have a safe neighborhood and good roads. Maybe they want clean water for washing, drinking, and bathing. They might not even all know each other, but they want some of the same things to make their lives more comfortable. Nevertheless, living near other people is only one type of community.

Alternative Communities

Many communities—in fact, most communities—are made up of people who don't consciously choose to live together. They just end up living near each other for other reasons. A person's neighbors may have moved into an apartment or a house because they liked it, because it was affordable, or because it was large enough for their entire family. Maybe it was close to where they work or to the school their children attend. They might even have chosen to live there because they like the neighborhood. Maybe they thought the people were friendly and responsible.

Some people choose to live in a certain area to be near people of the same ethnic background. Many cities, from Toronto to San Francisco, have neighborhoods with names like "Little Italy" or "Chinatown," areas where most of the people share the same ethnic origin. Living in this sort of community can help a person feel more comfortable and accepted. It may provide people with a greater social support network of people who share a common background.

Some people, however, desire more than just a passing acquaintance with their neighbors or a similar ethnic background. Some people have a deep desire to live with people with whom they share similar goals, ideals, and *ideologies*—not just similar ethnic backgrounds and *mundane* concerns.

People may come together to form a community dedicated to a shared vision or values. These sorts of communities are called *alternative communities*. Alternative communities have many of the same concerns and problems other communities experience—safety, taxes, sanitation, for example. Alternative communities, however, differ from *mainstream communities*—that is, from the general *populace*—in several important ways.

For one, alternative communities have some sort of theme, goal, or purpose. People may think that some mainstream towns and neighborhoods also have their own themes. Seattle, for example, touts itself as the "Emerald City," because it is known for its beautiful greenery and many gardens. This is a nice motto and it might describe Seattle well, but it isn't a theme in the same sense that an alternative community has a theme. While Seattle may be lush, the city itself does not have a purpose decided on by its inhabitants.

The purpose of an alternative community might be to try to live in harmony with nature. These sorts of communities are called *sustainable communities* or *eco-villages*. Another common type of alternative community focuses on religion or spirituality. In these communities, people might come together to pray or to help each other understand and explore their beliefs more fully.

Another characteristic common to alternative communities is a set of rules for all the community members that do not apply to people in mainstream society. These rules dictate how the people in the community are expected to live their lives while living in the community. In an eco-village, for example, residents may be required to

Residents of Taos Pueblo in New Mexico form an alternative community based on an ancient heritage. In the midst of the twenty-first century, they live in the same homes their ancestors did, without electricity or running water, practicing their people's religious ceremonies and traditional customs.

This postcard from the early twentieth century shows the quiet village of Lily Dale, an alternative community dedicated to the religious practices of Spiritualism. Because of the community's commitment to an alternative lifestyle, the village has changed very little in the past century.

use certain types of renewable energies such as solar power, or to only buy local goods when available.

A third common characteristic of alternative communities is that they tend to be quite small. This is partially due to the fact that most people do not want to spend the effort necessary to live in such a community. Though many people may want to help make the environment cleaner, few people seem to be willing to change their lifestyles to match the requirements of a sustainable community. More important, however, small communities are much easier to manage than large ones. Alternative communities are kept small for this reason.

Lily Dale

The idyllic town of Lily Dale in western New York is the perfect setting for an alternative community. It's beautiful, quiet, and out of the way. Lily Dale, known to many as the "spiritual hub of the Northeast," is home to a community of Spiritualists—people who believe that certain gifted people, called mediums, can communicate with the spirits of the dead. Because Lily Dale is dedicated to Spiritualism, it is an alternative community. However, that does not mean that the people of Lily Dale are exclusive or unwelcoming. In fact, during the summer months, the community regularly hosts guests interested in learning more about Spiritualism or in consulting with a medium.

Similar in nature to an alternative community is an *intentional community*. In fact, some people use the two terms interchangeably. Like an alternative community, an intentional community is one in which the members deliberately choose to live together to pursue common goals or purposes, or to live with people who share the same vision or values. Unlike alternative communities, however, intentional communities aim specifically to be self-sufficient or separated from mainstream society; alternative communities are more open to mainstream society.

For many intentional communities, this separation from the world is critical. In fact, for some, one purpose of the community is precisely that—separation from mainstream society. Like alternative

A Note About Terminology

What is normal or regular?

What is strange, odd, or weird?

We need to be careful using these words when we're talking about people who are different from ourselves. By saying that our community is normal, we are also saying that other communities are abnormal, or that there is something strange about them. But simply because something is different does not make it wrong, and it is important to respect the lifestyle choices people make. One way we can do that is to be aware of the words we use when talking about people who follow a different lifestyle than we do. People of different cultures, and many of the people who live in the intentional communities that we will be examining in this book, live alternative lifestyles. But that does not make them weird, strange, or abnormal—just different from most people.

communities, many intentional communities are based on common social ideals, such as environmentalism. Many others are based on common religious beliefs. In some cases, the beliefs that form the basis for the community require that it remain separate or isolated from the society at large.

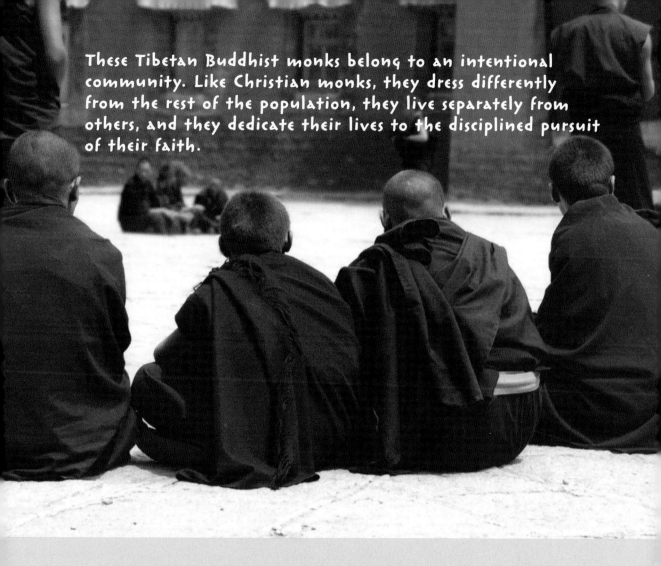

These Tibetan Buddhist monks belong to an intentional community. Like Christian monks, they dress differently from the rest of the population, they live separately from others, and they dedicate their lives to the disciplined pursuit of their faith.

We will be looking closely at the Amish, a group of people who share not only common religious beliefs that require this sort of separation, but a common ethnic heritage as well. The Amish are well known for living an extremely simple lifestyle. While their neighbors zoom around in cars and talk on cellular phones, the Amish still use horse and carriage to travel and are strictly forbidden from having phones in their homes. Despite their traditional ways and their reluctance to use technology, however, the Amish have carved a place for themselves in the modern economy.

CHAPTER 2
Origins of the Amish

In some rural villages, the Amish are a common sight in the grocery store parking lot on Saturdays. They park their horse and buggy in the corner, away from most of the cars, and set up a table spread with foods for sale. Home-baked breads, fresh vegetables from the garden, and fruit pies face the main road through town, enticing customers and passersby to stop and buy something. Out-of-towners often linger, eying the horses and buggies and the dark clothing. For many Americans, these glimpses of Amish life are like watching *Little House on the Prairie* or some other show about life before cars.

The Protestant Reformation

Today, just as it was three hundred years ago, tradition is one of the most important facets of Amish life. The history that forged those traditions is important to understanding the Amish today.

In the early sixteenth century, rising discontent in the Catholic Church led to a movement called the Protestant Reformation. At the time, almost all of Europe was Catholic, and the Catholic Church was extremely powerful. Many people believed that the Catholic Church and the pope had become corrupt, and that many of the Church's practices had strayed from the examples and commandments set forth in the Bible. The Protestant Reformation was an attempt by various religious leaders to try to reform, or change, the Catholic Church and its leadership.

The original goal of the Protestant Reformation was not to create a new *denomination*. Nevertheless, groups of people eventually split from the Catholic Church, because they realized that the Church would not change its ways. The members of these new Christian denominations became known as Protestants.

Early leaders of the Protestant Reformation protested against the Catholic Church over many issues. A prominent belief among the Protestants was that the Bible, not the Church, was the greatest source of moral authority and guidance. Protestants also objected to the role of priests as intermediaries, go-betweens, between God and the people. In other words, they believed that people themselves could form a close relationship with God and that priests should be little more than teachers and advisers.

Some Protestant denominations grew quickly, thanks to the support of kings and other political leaders who adopted a particular denomination as the official religion of their states. These leaders demanded that all people who lived in their country be baptized into the official state religion. For example, the *canton* of Zurich, in

Martin Luther is sometimes considered the father of the Protestant Reformation. A devout monk, he had no intention originally of starting a "new" religion; he merely wanted to bring his own faith back to what he believed were its true foundations.

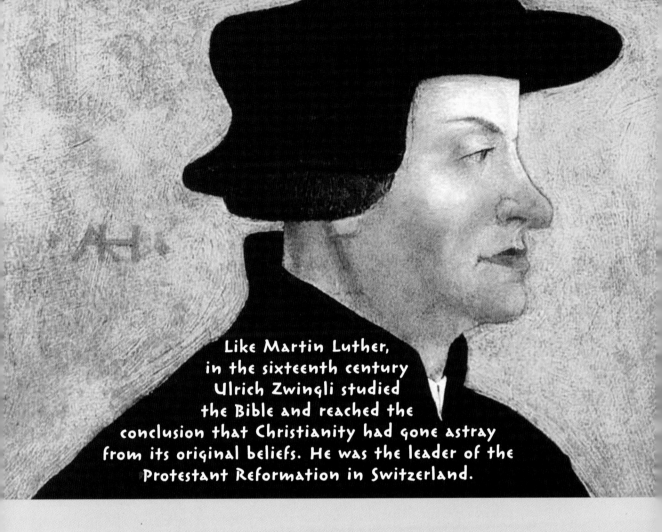

Like Martin Luther, in the sixteenth century Ulrich Zwingli studied the Bible and reached the conclusion that Christianity had gone astray from its original beliefs. He was the leader of the Protestant Reformation in Switzerland.

modern-day Switzerland, converted to the Swiss Reformed Church started by Ulrich Zwingli. Zwingli was so influential that the political leadership of Zurich ruled that all its citizens would have to be baptized into the church.

The Anabaptists

Despite the many differences between Catholicism and Protestantism, some people still felt the ties between the Church and the state undermined religion. Known as the Radical Reformers, these people wanted a complete separation of religion and govern-

The Significance of Baptism

In Christianity, baptism is a religious ritual meant to unite a person with Jesus Christ, and thereby cleanse the person of sin. The ritual, depending on the denomination of the person being baptized, may involve sprinkling or pouring water onto the head of the person, or it may involve completely immersing someone in water. For the Anabaptists, baptism was seen as a sacred and binding promise made between the individual and God, and could therefore only be made as an adult. For the state churches of the time, however, baptism was as much a legal ritual as it was religious. When a person was baptized, he became a citizen of the state, giving the state the power to tax him and to place him in military duty. Thus, by baptizing adults, the Anabaptists were showing their defiance of the church-states of the time.

ment. They also wanted church practices based even more rigidly on the words of the Bible than were the practices developed by other Protestant groups. Both the Catholic and Protestant churches based many of their practices on traditions that had developed after the Bible had been written. The Radical Reformers thought these traditions strayed from the commandments and teachings of the Bible; they wanted to return to the words of the Bible.

On January 21, 1525, a group of these reform-minded Protestants rebaptized each other, setting in motion the events that would lead to the formation of the Amish identity. This particular branch of the Radical Reformers came to be known as the Anabaptists, which means "rebaptizers" in Greek. At the time, people were usually baptized as infants. The Anabaptists, however, felt that young children, particularly infants, could not make an informed decision about their faith. Baptism, they believed, represented a promise to follow God and the teachings of the Bible. The Anabaptists believed only adults could truly and honestly choose to dedicate themselves to Christianity through baptism.

Almost immediately, the established institutions and authorities viewed the Anabaptists as a threat to the *status quo*. While the baptism of adults may seem like a harmless act, it had far-reaching implications in the society. Because religion and political power were so closely intertwined, a refusal to baptize one's children was viewed as a refusal to accept the government's authority. Baptism, in a sense, conferred citizenship. Baptizing adults, therefore, was like saying people had the choice of whether they wanted to follow the laws of the government. Clearly, this was unacceptable to the political authorities.

The Anabaptists also preached isolation from the rest of the world. In the eyes of the Anabaptists, there were two kingdoms—the Kingdom of God, to which they felt they belonged, and the kingdom of everyone else. To prevent the influences of the rest of the world from corrupting their own understanding of religion and morality, the Anabaptists withdrew from society and lived apart from other people. Again, this represented a threat to the political leadership, who believed the Anabaptists were trying to avoid military duty and taxes.

At the time, Europe was undergoing massive changes in every aspect of society. In addition to the religious turmoil of the Protestant Reformation, the economic and political maps of Europe were in constant flux, and power was shifting rapidly. Rulers and religious

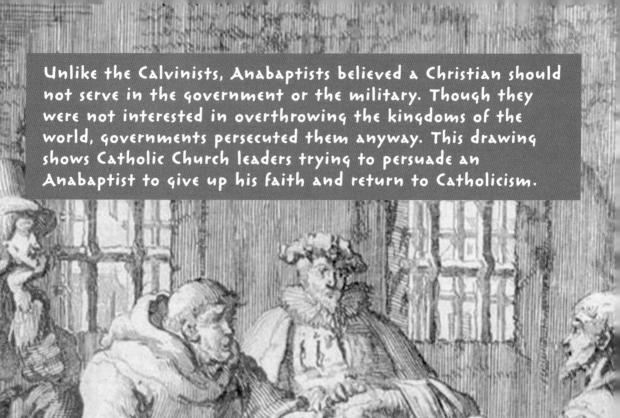

Unlike the Calvinists, Anabaptists believed a Christian should not serve in the government or the military. Though they were not interested in overthrowing the kingdoms of the world, governments persecuted them anyway. This drawing shows Catholic Church leaders trying to persuade an Anabaptist to give up his faith and return to Catholicism.

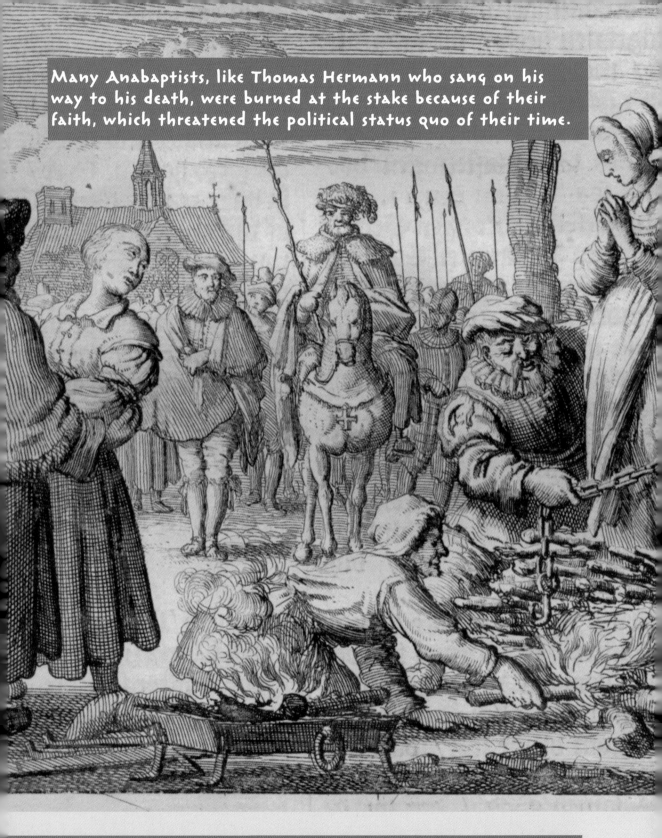

Many Anabaptists, like Thomas Hermann who sang on his way to his death, were burned at the stake because of their faith, which threatened the political status quo of their time.

The Martyr's Mirror

The Martyr's Mirror of the Defenseless Christians is a 1,100-page text describing the persecution and deaths of thousands of Anabaptist faithful. The book was written to remind Anabaptists of their heritage and history, and still serves as an inspirational guide to proper behavior and faith. The stories are simple but powerful. For example, one story recounts how Thomas Hermann was apprehended, tortured, sentenced to the fire, and burned. On his way to the place of execution, he composed and sang a hymn, which still exists. After Thomas Hermann, sixty-seven of his fellow believers were executed in the same place. Serving as a reminder of the demands God places on people's lives, The Martyr's Mirror is still an important text for Anabaptists today.

leaders found their authority challenged by the growth of a *mercantile* class in the expanding cities. Peasants rose up against their landlords and rulers. Thus, the political rulers and religious leaders of the time saw the actions and attitudes of the Anabaptists as dangerous—a possible *precursor* to rebellion. Because of this, the European Anabaptists suffered terrible persecution and retreated even further from mainstream society.

Important Figures in Amish History

Menno Simonszoon (Simon's son) was so influential that his followers came to be called Mennonites, after his own name. Menno had originally been a Catholic priest. Soon after his brother Pieter, an Anabaptist, was killed for his beliefs, Menno decided to be rebaptized. His zeal after his conversion helped to sustain the Anabaptist movement despite the harsh persecution it faced. His focus on nonviolence also became a feature of both Mennonite and Amish ideology.

Jakob Ammann was a tailor who contributed tremendously to the development of the Amish identity. In addition to advocating strict shunning of former church members, Ammann's skill in producing clothing led to the Amish use of hooks and eyes rather than buttons on coats and vests. This helped distinguish the Amish from the Mennonites, and is still a feature of Amish clothing throughout North America.

The **Martyr's Mirror** tells the story of Dirk Willems, an Anabaptist who was being chased by a "thief-catcher," sent by the local government to imprison him. When his pursuer fell through the ice, Willems turned around and rescued him. The thief-catcher pleaded that Willems' life be spared because of the courage and mercy he had shown, but the magistrates put Willems to death because of his faith.

The Mennonites and the Emergence of the Amish

Many Anabaptists fled to Switzerland and the Netherlands to escape persecution. By 1544, Dutch Anabaptists were starting to be called *Mennists* or *Mennonites*, after one of their early leaders, Menno Simonszoon. Simonszoon believed in total nonviolence. He believed the Bible strictly forbid the use of violence, as particularly shown by the example set by Jesus Christ in the Bible. Because of this, and because of their skill at making even poor soil productive, the Mennonites were able to find some rulers who invited them into

Menno Simonszoon (also known as Menno Simons) was the founder of the Mennonites, from which the modern Amish evolved. Like Martin Luther, Menno Simonszoon was a Catholic monk who sought to bring his faith back to life in a new way. His conviction that violence offers no permanent answers shaped his followers' lives down through the centuries.

their countries, including Czar Catherine the Great of Russia and Queen Elizabeth I of England.

While these arrangements helped save the Mennonites from further persecution, they also introduced certain difficulties into their lives. In many areas, harsh laws were passed that severely limited the freedom and comfort of the Mennonites. However, the Mennonites prospered in many other areas. Their prosperity may have been the greatest danger to the Mennonite way of life, which focused on living a simple life separated from the temptations of the outside world.

In 1693, conservative leaders of the Mennonite Church called for greater discipline in the church. Specifically, they wanted to halt what they saw as increasing worldliness and corruption. They sought to impose a strict ban against people who left the church after being baptized, preventing them from associating with other members of the church and community. The practice of banning former church members was not new to the Mennonite Church, but it had not been strictly implemented for various reasons. One of the chief reasons was because many former members of the Mennonite Church acted as intermediaries to the local governments on behalf of the church.

Jakob Ammann led the conservative reformers. Unable to convince the rest of the Mennonite Church to change its ways, he and a group of his followers split from the church. This splinter group of Mennonites became known as the Amish, named after their first leader.

Continued persecution in Europe eventually forced most of the Amish to leave for the New World. Beginning in the early eighteenth century, large numbers of Amish immigrants arrived in the colony of Pennsylvania, which was widely known for its religious tolerance. The Amish established communities in south-central Pennsylvania, near what is now Lancaster.

By 1900, most of the European Amish had either immigrated to North America or rejoined their Mennonite cousins. On January 17,

An Amish woman in Lancaster County, Pennsylvania, rides her bicycle into town. The Amish do not own cars, and they wear plain, old-fashioned clothing. These outward differences that set them apart from the rest of society are signs of their spiritual values and their intense commitment to their religious beliefs.

1937, the last Amish congregation in Europe joined a local Mennonite congregation. The Amish no longer live in Europe; they can only be found in the United States and Canada.

The Amish Today

After first settling in Pennsylvania, the Amish now live in twenty-five American states and in Ontario, Canada. This geographic spread reflects the high rate of population growth among the Amish. At the beginning of the twentieth century, the Amish population in North America was no larger than five thousand. Today, there are more than 180,000 Amish in more than 250 settlements in the United States and Canada.

Because the Amish first settled in Pennsylvania, they are often referred to as the "Pennsylvania Dutch." This name, however, is somewhat misleading. Most of the Amish are actually of German descent rather than Dutch, though there are also French, Swiss, and Welsh Amish in smaller numbers. The mistake apparently came from the similarity between the words "Dutch" and "Deutsch" (pronounced "doytch"), which is the German word for "German." In most Amish homes, people speak a *dialect* of German known as Pennsylvania German. Amish people learn English to interact with their non-Amish neighbors and use High German for their church services.

In addition to a shared language, several other features are characteristic of all Amish people. Perhaps most noticeable are their plain dress and their reliance on horses for transportation and fieldwork. You aren't likely to see an Amish person wearing the latest fashionable jeans or any sort of jewelry. Nor are you likely to see an Amish person driving around town in a car or truck. Rather, if you see an Amish person in town, he or she will probably be driving a horse-drawn buggy and will be wearing very plain homemade clothing.

Because of this, and because they reject most uses of electricity, the Amish appear to have changed little since their arrival in North

In many ways, the Amish seem like time travelers from the 1800s, and yet they move through the twenty-first century, abiding by modern traffic laws.

America during the eighteenth and nineteenth centuries. While people around them drive past in cars and trucks, the Amish still travel by horse and buggy. Most families in North America flip a switch to turn on the lights in their homes; the Amish light kerosene lamps. Many teens watch for the newest fashions in clothing and shoes, yet today Amish children wear essentially the same types of clothing as Amish children wore fifty years ago.

In an age when most children grow up using computers and watching television and DVDs, the Amish reject such technology. And yet the Amish are not only surviving but are actually thriving despite the fast pace of life around them. The Amish understanding of community is the key reason for this.

CHAPTER 3
Ordnung—Rules and Discipline

What do Amish boys and girls think when they see other young people listening to iPods as they walk around town? Do they wonder what it's like to hear music in their ears? Are they curious about the clothes they see, blue jeans and T-shirts?

Children from mainstream culture often have the same questions about the Amish: Do they get hot in those clothes? And why do they wear them in the first place? What do they do for fun?

Although different groups may dress and act differently, young people everywhere have fun doing many of the same things—playing games, talking, and laughing with their friends. People from different communities aren't so different after all.

The Role of Rules

If we think about it, we can see that all communities have certain rules and standards. Rules allow people with different needs and wants to interact with each other safely and productively. In a town, for instance, people must drive more slowly than they would drive on a highway. This is necessary because towns are full of people who are likely to be doing things like crossing the street or pulling their cars out of their driveways. In the same way, in university residence halls, students must be quiet after a certain hour so other students can study or sleep. Every community has rules.

The rules of an intentional community such as the Amish, however, dictate a far broader range of behaviors and help to set the community apart from mainstream society. The Amish have a specific name for their rules—the *Ordnung*. "Ordnung" is a German word that translates roughly into "rules and discipline." The Ordnung are unwritten rules that cover every aspect of Amish life— from religious rituals and family life to technology, dress, and leisure. More so than in most other communities, the Amish Ordnung is extremely important for the identity, growth, and vitality of the Amish community.

Although the Amish have spread out across North America, each individual community decides on its own rules. There is no central governing committee or board that rules over all Amish communities. Thus, the Amish community in Aylmer, Ontario, might have different rules from the Amish community in Sarasota, Florida. It is important to keep this in mind when making generalizations about the Amish. Saying that no Amish people ever use electricity, for example, is incorrect. While it may be correct for Amish in some communities, it is not true for all Amish everywhere.

Despite the small differences, certain similarities exist among all Amish congregations or communities. Although these commonalities cover a broad range of behaviors and expectations, we will

Even though an Amish woman may have a job in town, away from her community, she carries with her a clear sense of who she is and what she is allowed to do.

consider only three general categories of rules: rules governing a person's appearance, rules governing the ownership and usage of technology, and rules governing tradition and home life.

Rules Governing Appearance

Regardless of whether they live in Wisconsin or New York, all Amish people wear plain clothing. There are variations in colors and patterns from place to place, but in all cases, Amish clothing is meant to be functional rather than fashionable. Unlike many children in mainstream society, Amish children don't have separate clothes for play. The same clothes are worn for working in the barn as for playing in the yard. That's not to say that all Amish clothing is exactly the same. Mothers will make special clothing for going to church or school, and for special occasions like weddings. In general, however, even the nicest Amish clothes would be considered plain by mainstream standards.

In fact, in any given community, most people will be wearing clothes that look very similar. In many mainstream schools, you are likely to see many different styles of clothing. Some people may wear jeans, while others wear khakis. Some people might wear a sweater, while others wear a short-sleeved shirt. At an Amish school, however, all the girls wear dresses, aprons, and prayer caps; the boys wear pants, shirts, and vests.

The clothing that the Amish wear now has changed very little in design over the years. Still, there have been some changes. In some places, many of the young people—and even a few adults—occasionally wear sneakers. Though sneakers have been a common sight in most North American schools for decades, they are a fairly new addition to the Amish wardrobe and still forbidden in many communities. Buttons are still forbidden on men's coats, just as they were

An Amish family's dark clothing hangs on the line to dry. These clothes look very similar to what the family's ancestors wore a hundred or even two hundred years ago.

This Amish woman's clothing—the apron she wears over her dress and the special hat on her head—proclaims her identity as a member of a special community, separate from the rest of North American society.

Amish Wedding Rings

No one will find class rings at Amish schools. Amish men and women don't even wear engagement rings or wedding rings. That's because personal decorations like jewelry and body piercings are strictly prohibited among the Amish. Instead of wearing a wedding ring, an Amish man will begin to grow a beard (but never a mustache) when he is married. Thus, if an Amish man is without a beard, we know he is single.

Women also have a way of showing if they are married. Amish girls begin wearing a special apron over their dresses when they are about eight years old. During church services, unmarried girls wear a white apron, signifying virginity, while married women wear a black apron.

when Jakob Ammann first required hook-and-eye fasteners in 1693. However, these traditional fasteners have been replaced by snaps and nonornamental buttons on other items of clothing, such as trousers and shirts.

To many observers, these sorts of *minute* distinctions may seem contradictory. Certainly, Amish clothing styles do not change as quickly as mainstream clothing styles. The same can be said for the speed at which the Amish adopt new technologies. Just as they did when they first immigrated to North America, the Amish still rely on horses for transportation and fieldwork.

A World Without Electricity

Consider your daily routine for a moment. How often do you watch television? Play video games or use a computer? Listen to music on a stereo? How often do you use a refrigerator or microwave oven? How often do you turn on the lights? These things require electricity, an invisible force that has made modern living possible. And yet, what happens when we don't have electricity—for example, when the power is out because of a storm? Then we truly realize how dependent mainstream society has become on electricity. Imagine what your life would be like without ever having electricity. How would it be different? How might it be the same? What would you do for fun? When would you go to bed? You might be surprised to find that life without electricity really isn't as hard as you might have thought.

Rules Governing Technology

Horses still pull the buggies that are the mainstay of Amish transportation, even as ever-more advanced cars race past them. On the farm, Amish horses are still put to work in the fields, towing the plows and hay balers that are generally pulled behind powerful tractors on non-Amish farms. Because the horse is such an important part of life in an Amish household, children learn how to feed, care

Horses play an important role in the daily life of the Amish, just as these animals did a hundred years ago for all North Americans. In a world without electricity or gasoline engines, horses provide transportation.

This Amish community in Pennsylvania does not use electricity to light its homes, nor gasoline engines to power their wagons and farm machinery—and yet the Amish are permitted to use power tools and electricity outside of their own homes and farms.

for, and handle the horses at an early age. This responsibility is taken very seriously.

Just as the Amish forbid ownership of cars and tractors, they also do not allow electricity from public utility lines to be used in their homes, shops, and barns. Nor can Amish people have televisions or computers. Obviously, without electricity, computers and televisions would do the Amish little good even if they could own them.

It would be incorrect to say the Amish do not make use of any technology. In fact, the Amish use modern technologies in several ways. To many outside observers, the distinctions between banned technologies and accepted technologies can sometimes be rather confusing.

While electricity from public utility lines is strictly forbidden, many Amish communities allow the use of batteries. Although the Amish still light their homes with kerosene lamps, flashlights are acceptable in most communities. Amish buggies traveling at night are required by law to be equipped with lights powered by car batteries. Amish people in some other communities can avoid the potentially dangerous nighttime horse-and-buggy journeys by riding in a non-Amish neighbor's car, though they can never drive or own a car of their own.

In some other ways, Amish people actually use fairly sophisticated technology. In the Elkhart-Lagrange settlement in Indiana, for example, many young Amish people work in rural factories, many owned and operated by non-Amish businesspeople. In many other settlements, Amish carpenters are allowed to use power tools when they work on non-Amish houses. Those same carpenters, however, generally cannot use power tools to work on their own homes or on projects within the Amish community. In other places, hydraulic (liquid pressure) and pneumatic (air pressure) power replace electric or gas-combustion power. Thus, woodworking and metalworking equipment such as lathes, presses, and drills can still be used in some Amish workshops and factories.

Rules Governing Tradition

Although rules governing the traditions of the Amish are perhaps not so visible as those concerning technology and appearance, they are nevertheless important in shaping the identity of the Amish people. Again, while there may be some small differences here and there depending on the community in which an Amish person lives, there are still certain regularities between all of the Amish communities in North America.

For one, all Amish people speak Pennsylvania German at home. This traditional language, preserved from the early days of the Amish in Europe, helps the Amish people maintain their distinctive identity. Only a very few groups of people, including the Amish and Old Order Mennonites, speak this language in North America.

Another common feature of the Amish is the fact that their church services (held every two weeks) are held in people's homes. They have no central church building where they congregate on church Sundays. For this reason, every family must have a house large enough to hold all of the members of the congregation community. In some Amish settlements, this means that a house or barn must be large enough to hold more than one hundred people.

One tradition that has drawn a great deal of criticism over the years from mainstream observers holds that Amish children should not be educated beyond the eighth grade. While there are a few exceptions, almost all families obediently follow this rule. Though Amish teens finish with their schooling in the eighth grade—usually at the age of thirteen—they are not actually finished with their educations. Many enter practical apprenticeships, learning trade skills that will become their jobs as adults. For some teens, this means they begin working a full-time job when they are thirteen or fourteen years old.

These Amish teenagers may be done with school, but their training will continue as they learn the trades they will practice as adults.

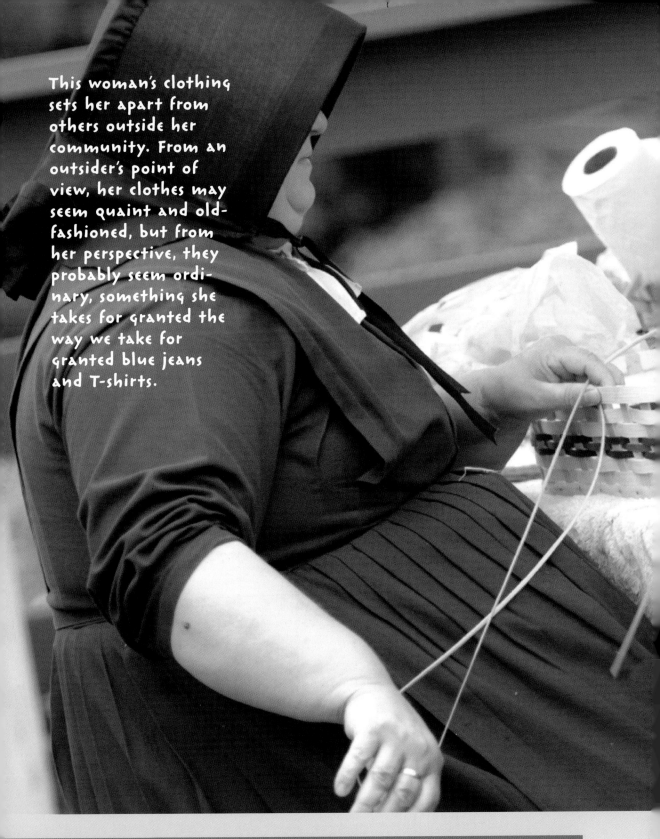

This woman's clothing sets her apart from others outside her community. From an outsider's point of view, her clothes may seem quaint and old-fashioned, but from her perspective, they probably seem ordinary, something she takes for granted the way we take for granted blue jeans and T-shirts.

Why All These Rules?

To many outsiders, the rules of the Amish might be a bit hard to understand. After all, why should Amish teens be forbidden to play video games and watch television when their non-Amish neighbors just down the road can? Even more confusing, why can an Amish carpenter use power tools when he is working away from home, but be unable to use them when he is working at home? It sometimes seems like many of the Amish rules are not just confusing, but that they contradict themselves.

If the rules themselves seem to form a crazy quilt of mismatched limitations and expectations, at least the purpose behind them is simple. Every rule in the Amish Ordnung has the same fundamental purpose—to help maintain the cultural and religious identity of the Amish.

Just as wearing the same uniforms helps unite a baseball or hockey team, the limitations on how Amish people dress bring them together as a community. The simple act of dressing alike gives all the people in an Amish community a shared identity. For teens, it helps avoid the natural competition for whom can get the latest fashions first. Again, just as hockey uniforms automatically separate players of one team from players of another team, Amish dress helps to separate Amish people—particularly Amish youth—from people in mainstream society.

Similarly, the rules governing Amish use of technology help to shield the Amish from influences in mainstream society that might corrupt their religious or cultural ideals. Some things, like calculators and electric welders, are acceptable because they help the Amish remain productive and financially competitive with their non-Amish neighbors without affecting the Amish sense of community. Some other technologies, like radios and televisions, would have a profoundly negative impact on Amish community, and so are banned. Such exposure to the outside world might tempt young

Some Amish communities—like this one in Lancaster County, Pennsylvania—allow its members to use bicycles. Other communities, however, prohibit even these engine-less vehicles.

people to leave the community, thus threatening the very existence of that lifestyle. Still others, like tractors and washing machines, would give Amish people an excess of idle time, which could lead to boredom and discontent with the Amish lifestyle.

Some other technologies that don't seem to be hazardous to the Amish way of life are forbidden for symbolic purposes. The prohibition on buttons, for example, is purely symbolic, a legacy of the rift that developed between the Mennonites and Amish in 1693.

Each time a new technology is introduced to the Amish, community leaders consider the technology, its uses, and how it might affect the community. They then decide, community by community, whether to accept the new technology or forbid it. For that reason, some communities allow their members to have bicycles, while others do not. The result, even within a single community, is a patchwork of acceptable technologies that may not make sense to an outsider. Indeed, it doesn't always make sense, even to many Amish. But not everything in mainstream culture always makes sense either.

Why, for example, do professional athletes make hundreds of thousands of dollars every year, while teachers and police officers do not? Why do cars and bicycles drive on the right side of the road in North America? Why should a person's belt match his shoes? Most people wouldn't know the answers to questions like these about their own culture, just as many Amish people wouldn't know the answers to questions about their own traditions. Still, there is an answer, which often lies deep within the traditions and history of a people. The Amish simply believe it is more important to respect their tradition than it is to question and analyze it.

CHAPTER 4
Choosing the Amish Lifestyle

Do Amish boys know that non-Amish boys go to baseball practice and get up on Saturday mornings to watch cartoons? Do Amish girls ever dream of driving cars when they grow up? Did they ever want to stop being Amish?

What about you? Do you ever look at your family's traditions and wish you could live your own life differently? Do you think, *When I grow up I won't do this—and instead I'll do that*? Eventually, when you leave home and become financially independent, you will be able to act on these questions. Amish teenagers get to make the same choices. Just like teenagers in mainstream society, however, many factors influence that decision, even if the teenagers don't realize it.

Amish Upbringing

Amish children start school at about the same age as other children in mainstream North American society, usually at four or five years of age. That is not to say that Amish children—or any children, for that matter—don't start learning until then. In fact, much of the learning that occurs in our lives takes place while we are still very young.

Think about it. By the time a child is ready to start school, she can walk, talk, run, play games with other children, and put on her clothes. Many children can already count, and some can even read by the time they start going to school. The brain of a young child is constantly developing, allowing children to learn things incredibly quickly.

Without even realizing, children everywhere learn their own language and culture—from the rules that their parents set for them to the examples set by the people around them. Even from a young age, a child's mother or father probably doesn't need to tell her that she should be nice to other people, or that she must wait until after dinner to have ice cream. People learn these things naturally, simply by growing up. It is these very sorts of unwritten rules children learn that form the basis for culture. Children learn the rules of their own culture from an early age. This is as true of Amish children as it is of children in other communities throughout the world.

Upbringing, or the way we learn the rules of our parents and our culture, happens naturally in all communities. How it happens, and how it influences people as they grow up, however, varies from one place to another, and from one culture to another. Differences exist between how Amish parents raise their children and how many non-Amish parents raise their children.

Generally, Amish families tend to be quite large. The motivation for this is quite simple—children provide extra hands to work around the house and on the farm. In fact, before the *advent* of machines like automatic hay balers and corn harvesters, farm families

Amish children—like all children—absorb their culture from the moment they are born. Having no electricity, dressing a certain way, and living in a special community all seem perfectly normal to a child who has grown up surrounded by Amish daily life.

in general tended to be quite large, whether Amish or not. Since 1900 alone, the average household size in the United States has fallen from 4.6 people per household to roughly 2.5 people per household.

In addition, Amish communities tend to be quite small—usually between twenty-five to forty families. In many Amish communities, families live in close proximity to their aunts, uncles, and cousins. Both figuratively and literally, Amish people often think of their Amish neighbors as family. These two factors—large families and tight-knit communities—provide young Amish people a very close network of friends and family with whom they interact on a regular

Amish children experience firm discipline from an early age. Humility and obedience are important character traits in Amish communities, so they are instilled at a very early age.

basis. Amish people generally know every person in their community very well, providing a greater degree of social security than what is found in many non-Amish communities.

This arrangement creates a much broader concept of family than that practiced in most non-Amish communities. Amish parents feel free to trust the welfare and development of their children to any of their neighbors, knowing that all the members of the community were raised in the same traditions and mindsets. Thus, if a child misbehaves, any adult in the community may discipline him for it.

The Amish take discipline quite seriously. Children are expected to be quiet, obedient, cooperative, and humble. Through the examples set by their parents and by older children around them, children

Gelassenheit

An important concept in Amish culture is the practice of Gelassenheit, self-surrender. It is based on the example of Jesus Christ as set forth in the Bible. Gelassenheit stresses humility, obedience, and the acceptance of life's difficulties as important virtues for all Amish people. Children learn Gelassenheit from a very young age, sometimes with a firm spanking if they are showing off. The following verse from the Amish publication The Instruction of Youth illustrates the ideals of Gelassenheit quite well:

I must be a Christian child,

Gentle, patient, meek, and mild;

Must be honest, simple, true

In my words and actions too.

I must cheerfully obey,

Giving up my will and way.

learn that respect and obedience to their elders are two of the most important virtues they must practice. Failure to obey can result in a slap or a spanking.

In many ways, the ideal Amish child is very different from mainstream society's image of the perfect child. Toys that reward toddlers with flashing lights and happy songs promote discovery and exploration, and toys that mimic musical instruments or that allow children to make pictures promote self-expression. Even if such toys could be made without electrical components, many Amish parents would likely never permit their children to play with such things. To Amish parents, allowing their children to have such toys would detract from the social contact between parent and child, and could foster characteristics in the children that would run contrary to the ideals of the Amish community.

Amish Education

Once an Amish child reaches five years of age, she is sent off each day to school, just like children in mainstream North American society. A few Amish children are sent to rural public schools, but most attend small, one-room schools. The Amish community usually builds these schools themselves, making the schools far less expensive than the large public schools many mainstream children now attend. Even though most Amish children do not attend public schools, Amish parents still must pay school taxes in most communities.

Children attend school through the eighth grade, mingling throughout the school day with children in all the other grade levels. Despite the wide range of ages and grade levels in the classroom, only one teacher—and perhaps a teacher's aide or two—moves around the classroom, instructing small groups of students for several minutes, giving them work to do, and then moving on to the next group. Older students often help younger students with their

The interior of a one-room Amish school house looks very like the mainstream schools of the nineteenth century. Amish education stresses cooperation—everyone working together—rather than competition—where each individual tries to do better than the others.

work. With all this activity, the classroom is generally a very busy place.

Nevertheless, the teachers keep the schools well ordered. The students, brought up to respect their elders and authority figures, usually behave for their teacher. Still, like many larger mainstream public schools, playful pranks are common in the classroom when the teacher isn't looking.

Amish pupils learn arithmetic, English, High German (as opposed to the Pennsylvania German they speak at home), history, and a smattering of geography and science. The Amish curriculum stresses cooperation over competition. Teachers reward hard work,

Wisconsin v. Yoder

In the nineteenth century, Amish children sat beside their non-Amish classmates in one-room public schools without incident. Starting in 1925, however, several trends in education began to worry the Amish. Many states began to close the one-room schools in favor of larger public schools, often requiring students to be bused to schools miles away. Lengthening school years and rising ages for compulsory school attendance also worried the Amish. They feared their children would be exposed to corrupting influences in the mainstream society and would not want to remain farmers. Finally, in 1972, the U.S. Supreme Court ruled that the Amish and several other religious groups were exempt from these requirements and could continue to operate their one-room schools. They ruled that attendance at public high schools would threaten Amish freedom of religion, which is protected by the Constitution.

kindness, and an interest in the subjects taught. Independent thought and critical analysis—the sort of questioning that many mainstream teachers try to encourage in their students—are frowned on. Such questioning is not highly regarded among the Amish, who prefer tradition to change. Nevertheless, tests taken by Amish and non-Amish students alike show that the Amish students do just about as well as their mainstream counterparts in those subjects they have in common.

Each school day is broken by a recess break. If the weather is nice, the students go outside to play, just as students in mainstream schools do. Amish games, like the Amish school curriculum, usually focus on cooperation and teamwork. Amish children play softball or volleyball during their recess break. In the winter, they may play in the snow, go sledding, or even go skating on a nearby pond.

After school, children return home to do their chores. From an early age, Amish boys and girls are expected to work around the house and the farm. Children learn how to care for the farm animals, such as cows and horses. They are also expected to clean and do other chores as necessary. This sort of informal education may be more important for the Amish than the subjects they learn in school, because these are the chores that prepare the Amish young for the lives they will likely lead in the future.

Rumspringa

Amish children finish their schooling with completion of the eighth grade. They don't graduate in the way that most mainstream students understand graduation. While an Amish student may get some congratulations after finishing his schooling, there is unlikely to be a great deal of pomp and celebration surrounding the event, largely because the Amish avoid displays of pride. One of the more frequently quoted verses of the Bible among the Amish when they are speaking of education comes from 1 Corinthians 8:1: "Knowledge puffs up [makes us arrogant] but . . . anyone who claims to know something does not yet have the necessary knowledge."

Amish teens are usually thirteen years old when they finish their schooling. At that point, many of them go to work, usually either at home or for a relative. Girls are given responsibilities at home, while boys are sometimes allowed to go to work in Amish workshops and

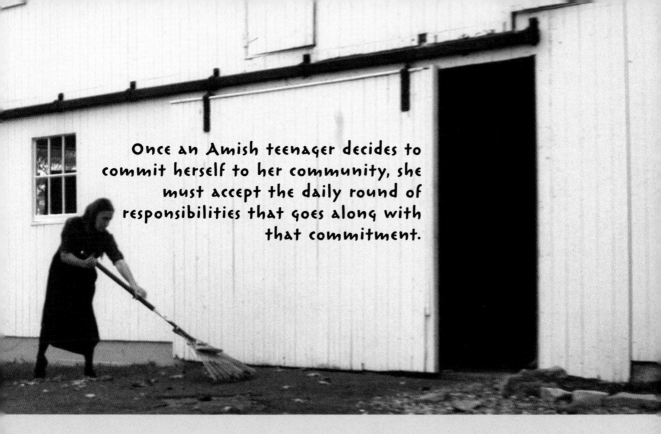

Once an Amish teenager decides to commit herself to her community, she must accept the daily round of responsibilities that goes along with that commitment.

factories. For both boys and girls, it is a time to start learning the specific skills they will need to be productive in their community.

Although the young teens are given more responsibilities at home, and may even have full-time jobs, they are not considered adults. They must still obey their parents and do as they are told. When they turn sixteen, however, teenagers gain a much greater degree of freedom.

Among the Amish, the sixteenth birthday is an important milestone. At this age, an Amish teenager is considered old enough to decide for herself whether she would like to be baptized, thereby joining the Amish church. As Anabaptists, the Amish baptize their members only as adults, so they have the option not to be baptized. In essence, they have the option not to become Amish themselves. Beginning at age sixteen, young Amish people are given the freedom to explore their world to discover whether they themselves would like to become Amish.

Amish in the City

In July 2004, cable station UPN debuted a new reality television show called <u>Amish in the City</u>, which focused on five young Amish people during Rumspringa who had been lodged in a house in the Hollywood Hills with six city-dwelling housemates. Cameras followed the young Amish people as they experienced "English" culture, apparently for the first time. In the end, all five of the Amish people in the show decided to remain in the "English" world rather than return to their Amish roots. However, some critics felt that the show—which introduced the Amish to many unusual experiences, such as parasailing—did not present a realistic view of the modern world to the young Amish, possibly skewing their decisions.

This period in their life is called *Rumspringa*, which means literally "running around" in German. It is the time in a young Amish person's life when he can "run around" and experience the life of a non-Amish person. During this period, many parents allow their children to do things normally forbidden among the Amish.

The teens may dress "English," wearing the clothing of mainstream society, such as jeans and T-shirts. Boys might buy a car when they are eighteen, though girls very rarely do. In some cases, young people might even experiment with alcohol and drugs. In 1998, two Amish teens were arrested after being caught dealing cocaine. The story made national headlines, and was prominently featured in such magazines as *The New Yorker* and *Time*.

Such extremes are rare, however. Most Amish teenagers never stray far from their upbringing. For them, Rumspringa is a time to travel to other nearby Amish settlements and make new friends. During this time, most Amish teens begin dating. Many become baptized only after they have found the person they want to marry.

Baptism

Despite the temptations of the outside world—television, cars, music, clothing—most Amish teens in Rumspringa choose to return to the Amish church and be baptized as members. In fact, 85 to 90 percent will join the church. This may seem surprising. However, several factors make baptism and the return to the Amish lifestyle much more appealing.

For one, Amish teenagers only have an eighth-grade education. Without at least a high school education, their options are extremely limited. Few of them can find high-paying work, and what work they can find is often difficult and tedious—unskilled factory work, cleaning, or cooking, for example. Some live for a few years on their own, but eventually return to the church when they realize that they cannot compete for good jobs.

Another issue facing teenagers who decide not to pursue the Amish life is the loss of friendship. Everyone they have ever known is Amish. The close network of friends, neighbors, and family who surrounded them in their youth will be gone if they choose not to be Amish. This separation can be extremely painful and lonely, forcing many young people to return to the community.

Finally, there is the simple fact that the Amish lifestyle is an attractive one for many, particularly those raised in it. Life without television, cars, and electric lights is not necessarily a boring or bad life. Amish people enjoy a great deal of social contact; even when they are working, they are chatting, joking, and laughing. Many Amish youth see no reason why they shouldn't be baptized. They ap-

These Amish young people are "courting"—the term for what most of us would consider dating.

preciate the spiritual values and close relationships of the community where they were raised.

Still, a few decide they don't want the Amish lifestyle. These people become "English," adopting modern ways as their own. Although they are no longer members of the Amish community, in some cases, they may continue to maintain their ties with their old friends and family.

Those who accept baptism and then later leave the Amish church, however, can expect a different response from the people in their community. Just as they did in 1693 when Jakob Ammann led his followers to split from the Mennonites, the Amish believe in *shunning* those who stray from their faith. The Amish believe baptism is a sacred and binding promise not to be taken lightly. Other Amish treat those who break that promise as though they no longer exist. Family members leave the room when their sibling or child who broke the promise of baptism enters the room. Other community members avoid that person, refusing to speak to—or even look at—the shunned individual.

Shunning is the strongest punishment the Amish can use. As a punishment, it helps deter members from backing out on the vows they make through baptism, and it encourages people who are being shunned to rejoin the church and the Amish community. It is also used as a deterrent, helping members who are not being shunned to avoid any sorts of temptations the shunned individual might present. By avoiding the shunned individual, other community members also avoid any corrupting influences that individual might offer.

The goal of shunning, then, is not simply to punish the individual who breaks his baptismal vows. Rather, it is an attempt to try to maintain the integrity of the Amish community, just as the many rules of the Ordnung are intended to safeguard the identity of the community. While it may be an exaggeration to say that everything the Amish do is focused on their community, it is certainly accurate to say that their focus on their community sets them apart from the mainstream society around them.

Most of us think of our-
selves first as individuals
and second as members of
whatever community to
which we belong. This
woman, however, probably
thinks of herself first and
foremost as Amish. Her
community defines her
identity.

Rumspringa is only a brief period in an Amish individual's life. Most Amish young people eventually settle down within their communities.

Devil's Playground

Lucy Walker's documentary <u>Devil's Playground</u> follows several young Amish people from Indiana who are experiencing "English" life during their Rumspringa. Although the film's producers compare finding Amish youth willing to talk about their experience to finding a "needle in a haystack," the filmmakers were able to find several young people whose situations and experiences are memorable. Some examples:

Faron Yoder—son of an Amish preacher, Faron wants to become a preacher himself. First, however, he needs to overcome his drug habit and then decide whether he wants to be baptized or follow his girlfriend to Florida.

Velda Bontrager—a young woman who was baptized in the Amish church but then left is shunned by her family and friends.

Gerald Yutzy—a teenager who says he already knows he won't become Amish. By the end of the film, however, he has moved back in with his parents.

CHAPTER 5
Other Alternative Communities

The Amish live in what is perhaps the most well-known and most visible alternative community in North America. However, the discussion of alternative communities would be incomplete without looking at some of the other types of communities that exist.

Because alternative communities are established to promote a particular ideology or further a particular goal, the variety of communities is almost staggering. Not only do alternative communities have different goals, but they also organize their communities ways in a wide variety of ways. Often, these differences come down to the decisions of community members on how to achieve the goals of their communities.

Other Religious Communities

Religion pulls people together from many different backgrounds, and it has been a powerful force in producing alternative communities. In some cases, a *fervent* desire to connect with other people who share the same strong convictions can bring a community together. One example of this sort of religious community is a convent or monastery. These religious institutions are communities of people—nuns and monks—who are deeply devoted to their religion. In pursuit of their religious ideals, nuns and monks take solemn vows to dedicate themselves to their religion and to uphold high moral standards.

They do this in order to purify their lives and to grow in their understanding of their religion and their relationship with God. In medieval Europe, some orders of monks worked as scribes, copying and translating old books for libraries. Their work helped preserve much of the knowledge and philosophy of ancient Rome and Greece, civilizations that heavily influenced the development of European and North American culture.

Unlike many other types of communities, no children live in convents and monasteries. The nuns and monks who live in these communities must remain celibate and *chaste*; they cannot have children or families. In order to grow, new members of these communities must come from outside the community—usually adults whose faith draws them to the monastic lifestyle. Although there are not as many nuns and monks now as there were in the Middle Ages, some people still are interested in following this sort of lifestyle. Functioning convents and monasteries can still be found throughout the world.

One such monastery is the Abbey of the Genesee in Piffard, New York, a small town south of Rochester. The Abbey is home to the

Monks at the Abbey of the Genesee believe their faith is lived out through performing ordinary work—like baking the bread that also supports their community.

monks of the Cistercian Order of the Strict Observance—also known as the Trappists. These modern-day monks must really believe that "the early bird gets the worm": they start each day with a morning prayer session at 2:25 A.M., while most other people are still sleeping soundly. Their day ends before some people have even had dinner. At 6:35 P.M., the Trappists hold their final prayer session of the day, and then head off to bed.

In between those times, they read, pray, and work quietly in their bakery. Monks' Bread, made by the monks in the Abbey using state-of-the-art baking machinery, is sold in supermarkets all over western New York. Unlike their counterparts in the Middle Ages, the Trappists also have access to computers and the Internet.

Convents and monasteries are only one type of religious community; many other kinds attract people of every religious denomination. Some are even comprised of people from many different faiths. All religious communities share one thing in common, however: they unite people with similar interests and goals so they can share in each other's life experiences.

Communes

Another type of alternative community that is particularly effective in helping people share the meaningful experiences of life with other people is called a commune. Communes are social and economic communities that require members to share community resources and responsibilities. Typically, all people in a commune contribute to the financial well-being of the community, and in many cases they share the work that needs to be done to keep the community going. This work might include farming, building houses, cooking, or anything else the community needs.

Because communes allow members to share the cost of living with each other, these are one of the most common forms of alternative communities. Some communes are dedicated to a wide vari-

Kibbutzim

Comprising the largest secular, or nonreligious, commune movement in the world, <u>kibbutzim</u> are communes in Israel; 2 percent of the country's population live in kibbutzim. Members of a kibbutz (the singular form of kibbutzim) share all the foods and services of the community as needed. Like many communes, kibbutzim are governed democratically, with all members cooperating both in making decisions and in carrying out those decisions. Many factors in Israel led to the development of kibbutzim, including difficult economic times, a desire to celebrate and develop the Israeli identity, and a need to develop new lands to support a growing population. In return, kibbutzim have had a tremendous influence on Israeli history and national politics. As a communal movement, kibbutzim are one of the most successful in the world.

ety of different goals, including the preservation of the environment, military training, religious freedom, and political expression.

In the 1960s and 1970s, North America experienced an explosion in the number of communes being established. This was largely due to the hippie *countercultural* movement. The hippies advocated peace and brotherly love among all people. For many hippies, communes were a way to put their message of peace into practice. They

Many of Israel's fertile farms are owned and operated by kibbutzim.

believed a strong sense of community would develop in the communes because all members shared responsibility for their resources; because they were invested in the community, they would want the community to succeed. Strong communities, in turn, would lead to peace.

The Farm is one of the best-known communes to develop in North America. Established in 1971, the founders of The Farm wanted to create a place where people could live peacefully in harmony with nature. To that end, members of The Farm live a very simple lifestyle, not unlike the Amish. In fact, some Farm members began to call themselves "Amish in Technicolor," referring to the bright colors that were very characteristic of the hippies.

One of the goals of The Farm is to find creative new ways to diminish the impact that people have on the environment. Farm members look at the way homes are heated, the way water is used, and the amount of garbage produced, and they try to find ways to improve wasteful habits. One way they try to reduce their impact on the world is by practicing strict veganism. Farm members avoid eating or using anything made or taken from animals, including meat, eggs, milk, leather, and even honey. Instead of using animal products, they try to find substitutes from plants. Not surprisingly, Farm members grow much of their own fruits and vegetables. In fact, the community is self-sufficient in food production, meaning it produces enough food to feed all of its members.

Children on The Farm are also bound by this lifestyle. Just like their parents and other adults around them, the children are not allowed to eat or use any animal products. Of course, sometimes, if they had the opportunity, they would try to sneak a tasty treat that was otherwise discouraged. Rachel Meunier, who grew up on The Farm, related the story on The Farm's lifestyle Web site of how she and some other children found a wheel of cheese a relative had sent. While the adults discussed what they would do with the cheese, Meunier wrote, "The kids, myself included, managed to finish off the entire block of cheese before the issue was resolved."

Children also work alongside the adults, doing chores just like children do in most other communities. Those old enough often work with their parents and other adults in the gardens, or in any other area as needed—possibly working in a store serving Farm members. For the most part, then, life for children on The Farm is not so very different from life in many other communities—except that their life is built around a central goal.

The Farm's way of life is sometimes called a "sustainable" lifestyle, and is the goal of another type of alternative community called an eco-village. In fact, one source of income for The Farm is its Eco-village Training Center. This visitors' center showcases technologies and design techniques that people can use to reduce their

Eco-villages are committed to finding clean energy alternatives, such as solar power, which uses sunshine to provide heat for this home.

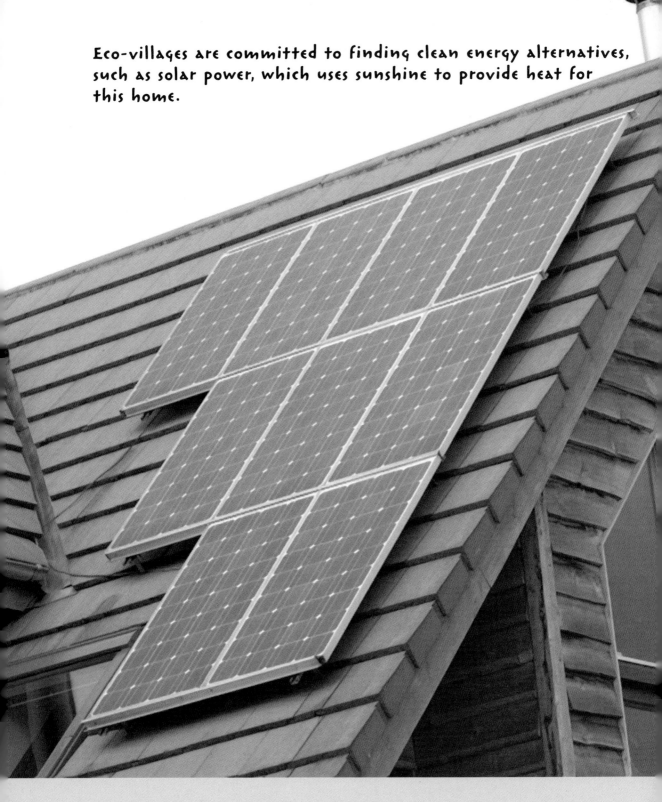

impact on the environment. Tourists visiting the Center can learn about energy-efficient hybrid fuel vehicles, solar power and passive solar heating systems, and building designs that help save energy.

The members discovered many other ways that they could make money to support their community. Many of the members work in nearby towns, while others work in the community itself. They all pay a reasonable rent, which is determined during meetings of the members. In addition, The Farm lodges several successful businesses in addition to the Eco-village Training Center. A book publishing business, a solar energy business, a soy food business, a medical clinic, an ambulance, a midwife service, and a senior citizens' center all help financially sustain The Farm while also providing socially and environmentally valuable services to the outside world.

Not all alternative communities are successful. These ruins were once a commune, back in the sixties, but its members have gone on to live other lives, most likely in mainstream society.

Failed Communities

Not all alternative communities withstand the test of time. Many fail, and for a wide variety of reasons. Some examples:

Hopedale, 1842–1856—This community, funded through stock owned by community members, went bankrupt when two members withdrew from the community, taking with them three-quarters of the community's stock and funding.

Brook Farm, 1841–1847—Due to poor soil and unskilled farmers, this experimental farm did not make enough money to survive an episode of smallpox in 1845 and a fire that destroyed the community's central building in 1846.

Oneida Society, 1848–1879—A utopian commune that believed in a great many radical ideas, the Oneida Society collapsed after its charismatic leader, John Noyes, died. The members reorganized their assets to form Oneida Limited, a producer of cutlery and flatware.

CHAPTER 6
Respecting Our Differences

Let's pretend that your friend gives you a food you've never tried before. Maybe you look at it and try to figure out how it tastes by its color. Maybe you smell it. Eventually, you take a bite. After all, you'll never know if you like it or not unless you try it.

The taste isn't bad—just strange. You've never tasted anything quite like it before, and really, you're just not sure if you like it. So what do you do then? Do you put it down and say you'll never eat it again? Or do you try it again, thinking that you might start to like it after you've gotten used to its taste?

Now let's say that you see an Amish boy standing in front of you. He's wearing his homemade pants and shirt, and a vest without buttons. What would you think? Would you think that his clothing looks strange?

It's okay if that's what you think, because sometimes when you see or try something new for the first time, it just seems strange. After all, it's different. In this case, he—the Amish boy—is different. Sometimes it takes a while to get used to people or things that are different from what we have experienced in the past.

Now, think back to the food your friend offered you. Did you decide to try it again, or did you decide that you never wanted another bite? If you try it again—if you take some time to get used to the taste—you're probably going to learn to like it. The same is true for people of different cultures and different backgrounds. If you give them a chance, you might find that you really like them.

Similarities

What would be the first thing that you noticed about the Amish boy standing in front of you? His straw hat? His homemade clothing? Maybe his vest with no buttons?

Many people first notice differences. That's just human nature. If you put two red balls and one green ball in a line, which ball will you look at first? Probably the green ball, because it's different from the other two balls.

So again, if you notice his clothing first, that's okay. That's just natural. The important thing is what you look for next.

Maybe the Amish boy is laughing at a joke one of his friends told him. Or maybe he's playing with some other Amish boys. Maybe he is reading a book or doing his homework. Maybe he is doing chores at home.

You may sometimes do these things, too. So maybe he isn't so different from you than you first thought. In fact, maybe if you took

When you meet people, what do you notice first? Whether they're male or female, young or old, a person of color or white? If you notice differences first, that's only normal—but the most important things are what we all have in common, regardless of our differences.

Ultimately, we all belong to a single global community!

some time to get to know him, you would discover that you have a lot in common with him. Sometimes it takes a while, but eventually you are almost certain to see some things that you have in common.

When you get right down to it, we're all similar in some very fundamental ways. For example, we all live in a community of some sort. We all learn certain rules and expectations while we're growing up in our community. And we all have feelings.

Respect

When we meet people who are different from ourselves, it is important to remember that they have good reasons for the way they look and act. Perhaps we can't understand the reasons, but that does not

Our Biases

A bias is an influence on the way we think about something. For example, a lawyer might say that a juror is biased by her past experience. That means the lawyer thinks some past experience is influencing the juror's thoughts on the case. Often, our biases negatively influence our thoughts about something. Furthermore, the way we are raised introduces influences we often don't realize are there. The same is true of our culture. We often like or dislike things because we learned to like or dislike them as a result of our upbringing or our culture. It's important for us to try to stop and think about why we react to new and different things the way we do. If we understand our biases, sometimes we can come to appreciate the differences around us much more easily.

make them wrong. Respect is the ability to see a person's differences and similarities, and then to accept that person as she is.

Just because you respect someone, however, does not mean that you need to agree with her all the time. It is possible to respectfully disagree with someone, and that is one of the most important skills anyone can learn. Living in communities as we do, we are constantly interacting with people, many of whom are different from ourselves. Rules help communities to remain ordered. Respect, however, is the basis for all these rules.

Further Reading

Bial, Raymond. *Visit to the Amish Country*. Urbana, Ill.: Phoenix Publishing, 2005.

Butterfield, Jim. *Driving the Amish*. Scottdale, Pa.: Herald Press, 1997.

Coleman, Bill. *The Gift to Be Simple: Life in an Amish Country*. San Francisco, Calif.: Chronicle Books LLC, 2001.

Davis, Martha Moore. *Sarah's Seasons: An Amish Diary and Conversation*. Iowa City: University of Iowa Press, 2000.

Garrett, Ruth Irene, and Ottie Garrett. *My Amish Heritage: The Pictoral Journey of Ruth Irene Garratt*. Paducah, Ky.: Turner Publishing Company, 2003.

Garrett, Ruth Irene, and Deborah Morse-Kahn. *Born Amish*. Paducah, Ky.: Turner Publishing Company, 2004.

Good, Phyllis Pellman. *Amish Children*. Intercourse, Pa.: Good Books, 2002.

Hastings, Robert J. *Samuel: The Inspiring Story of How an Amish Boy's Tragedy Brought Two Worlds Together*. Athens, Ga.: Longstreet Press, 1997.

Highsmith, Carol. *The Amish: A Photographic Tour*. New York: Random House Value Publishing, Inc., 1999.

Hurwitz, Laura, Amanda Lumry, Thom Lumry, and Loren Wengerd. *Holmespun: An Intimate Portrait of an Amish and Mennonite Community*. Bellevue, Wash.: Eaglemont Press, 2002.

Lewis, Beverly. *Just Like Mama*. Minneapolis, Minn.: Bethany House Publishers, 2002.

Lewis, Beverly. *Abram's Daughters: The Covenant*. Minneapolis, Minn.: Bethany House Publishers, 2002.

Lewis, Beverly. *Abram's Daughters: The Betrayal*. Minneapolis, Minn.: Bethany House Publishers, 2003.

Lewis, Beverly. *Abram's Daughters: The Sacrifice*. Minneapolis, Minn.: Bethany House Publishers, 2004.

Lewis, Beverly. *Abram's Daughters: The Prodigal*. Minneapolis, Minn.: Bethany House Publishers, 2004.

For More Information

Eco-villages
gen.ecovillages.org

The Farm
www.thefarm.org
www.thefarmcommunity.com

Intentional Communities
www.ic.org

Lancaster County Visitor Center
www.padutchcountry.com

Lily Dale
www.lilydaleassembly.com

Publisher's note:
The Web sites listed on this page were active at the time of publication. The publisher is not responsible for Web sites that have changed their addresses or discontinued operation since the date of publication. The publisher will review and update the Web-site list upon each reprint.

Glossary

advent: Arrival of something.

canton: A division of a country, much like a state.

chaste: Sexually pure.

countercultural: Descriptive of a culture with ideas and practices contrary to mainstream society.

denomination: A religious grouping within a faith.

dialect: The regional variety of a language.

fervent: Showing passionate enthusiasm for something.

ideologies: Sets of beliefs, values, and opinions that shape the ways individuals or groups think, act, and understand the world.

mercantile: Relating to merchants or trading.

minute: Extremely small in size or scope.

mundane: Commonplace, ordinary.

precursor: Somebody or something that comes before and is often considered to lead to the development of another person or thing.

populace: Inhabitants of a town, region, or other area.

shunning: Deliberately avoiding someone as a form of punishment.

status quo: The way things are now.

Bibliography

Brown, Susan Love. *Intentional Community: An Anthropological Perspective.* Albany: State University of New York Press, 2002.

Friesen, John W., and Virginia Lyons Friesen. *The Palgrave Companion to North American Utopias.* New York: Palgrave Macmillian, 2004.

Hoff, Marie D. ed. *Sustainable Community Development: Studies in Economic, Environmental, and Cultural Revitalization.* Boca Raton, Fla.: Lewis Publishers, 1998.

Janzen, William. *Limits on Liberty: The Experience of Mennonite, Hutterite, and Doukhobor Communities in Canada.* Toronto, Ont.: University of Toronto Press, 1990.

Kraybill, Donald B. *The Riddle of Amish Culture.* Baltimore, Md.: The Johns Hopkins University Press, 2001.

Kraybill , Donald B., and Carl F. Bowman. *On the Backroad to Heaven: Old Order Hutterites, Mennonites, Amish, and Brethren.* Baltimore, Md.: The Johns Hopkins University Press, 2001.

Rice, Charles S., and John B. Shenk. *Meet the Amish: A Pictoral Study of the Amish People.* Piscataway, N.J.: Rutgers University Press, 1947.

Tyldesley, Michael. *No Heavenly Delusion? A Comparitive Study of Three Communal Movements.* Liverpool, England: Liverpool University Press, 2003.

Zelinski, John M. *Amish Across America.* Dubuque, Iowa: Kendall Hunt, 1983.

Index

Picture Credits

Abbey of the Genesee: p. 75
Harding House Publishing, Ben Stewart: pp. 18, 32, 34, 36, 39, 41, 45, 46, 49, 52, 57, 64, 70
iStockphoto: pp. 8, 87
    Bootay, Steve: p. 58
    Brammer, Nancy: p. 54
    Donenfield, Mike: p. 78
    Frommer, Jill: p. 13
    Gascho, Mary: p. 69
    Hill, Rob: p. 81
    Lane, Catherine: p. 88
    London, Cat: p. 17
    McBeath, Steve: p. 10
    Monino, Juan: pp. 42, 50
    Pleasant, Tim: p. 82
    Stay, Mark: p. 84
    Warren, Sean: p. 72
    Wislander, Kenn: p. 61
Lingbeek-van Kanen, Klaas: p. 67
Mennonite Library and Archives, Bethel College: pp. 25, 26, 29

To the best knowledge of the publisher, all other images are in the public domain. If any image has been inadvertently uncredited, please notify Harding House Publishing Service, Vestal, New York 13850, so that rectification can be made for future printings.

Biographies

Author
David Hunter grew up in Amish country in western New York, where he learned an early appreciation for the Amish culture. More recently, he has returned from the Republic of Kiribati, where he served as a Peace Corps volunteer for two years. He has had several articles published in homeschooling magazines, and currently works and resides in Binghamton, New York.

Series Consultant
Celeste J. Carmichael is a 4-H Youth Development Program Specialist at the Cornell University Cooperative Extension Administrative Unit in Ithaca, New York. She provides leadership to statewide 4-H Youth Development efforts including communications, curriculum, and conferences. She communicates the needs and impacts of the 4-H program to staff and decision makers, distributing information about issues related to youth and development, such as trends for rural youth.